From Participants of AnamCara Clergy Groups

"With trusted friends, I was able to discover a perspective that once again compelled me to engage in the mystery of Christ and community. I was strengthened through silence, prayer, and dialogue to claim my calling."

—Nancy Sehested
Chaplain, Marion Prison

"I can no longer imagine doing pastoral ministry without my group of soul friends. Our time together often feels like a taste of the Kingdom, a feast of deep laughter and friendship among competent peers who respect each other. In a wonderfully paradoxical way, the worship, study and conversation we share make me a better pastor and remind me there is more to my life than ministry.

"During my cancer surgery and recovery, then the death of my Dad, the congregation I serve as pastor could not have been more supportive. But in a unique way that I cannot describe, my clergy group was a lifeline. Now that I'm back into my work, it remains a lifeline."

—Steve Hyde
Pastor, Ravensworth Baptist Church,
Anandale, Virginia

"Being rather untraditional in my understanding of church, I was skeptical at first. But a few months into our clergy meetings, I sent a message to a more established pastor in the group, 'I will always be grateful that a tall-steeple preacher and a fringey granola reverend set aside our preconceived notions and met at the altar of friendship.' What I thought would be most difficult turned out to be the greatest gift of our clergy circle. From the varied contexts as pastors and chaplains, we found common ground in silence and biblical reflection, in singing and sharing, in feasting and communion."

—Joyce Hollyday
UCC pastor of Circle of Mercy,
Asheville, North Carolina

"[By] being part of a clergy peer community I had the opportunity to hear and be heard as a community of colleagues gave voice to the joys and struggles, demands and opportunities, affirmations and questions which are part of the practice of ministry. We share laughter and tears, prayer and worship, new ideas and hard-won wisdom."
—Guy Sayles
Pastor, First Baptist Church, Asheville, North Carolina

"My experience in clergy community was thought-provoking, nourishing, a place to practice listening to God, to ourselves and to each other. Even when separated between gatherings, I felt their support and challenge in my daily rhythm of ministry."
—Anne Hunter Eidson
Minister of Music, Park Road Baptist Church,
Charlotte, North Carolina

"I was a member of an AnamCara clergy group for three years, commuting from Richmond, Va. to Raleigh, N.C. When I moved to northern Virginia, I helped to start a similar peer community. We are in our fifth year. It's integral to the way I practice ministry."
—Ben Wagener
Pastor of Spiritual Formation,
Vienna Baptist Church, Vienna, Virginia

"Participating in a clergy group has been soul-saving for me and my vocation. I know of no other support experience in which I can step out of my role and reflect upon it by receiving the collective wisdom of other 'practitioners' who are in the trenches with me."
—Rob Field
Rector, St. Philip's Episcopal Church

"As with most meaningful experiences, AnamCara is best appreciated in hindsight. It gave me access to trusted friends and in their company I could run something by them, debrief a pastoral situation, share a funny story, ask for feedback, share a meal, sit in silence together, hear the continuation of their stories (their families, their ministries, their own soul's journey). This group quickly embodied a sense of home for me."
—Amy Dean
Pastor, Park Road Baptist Church, Charlotte, North Carolina

Anam Cara
Collegial Clergy Communities

by
Mahan Siler

A note from the author: If you want to explore these collegial clergy groups, there are two ways to proceed.

One, CareNet of North Carolina, a network of faith-integrated counseling, has adopted AnamCara as an extension of its ministry. Also, through periodic training events, CareNet offers certification of AnamCara facilitators to those within and beyond North Carolina.

If you see either option as something you want to pursue, you may contact Bryan Hatcher, Director of Professional Services, CareNet, Inc., *bhatcher@wfubmc.edu* or a pastoral counselor within CareNet known to you.

Secondly, you may contact me through my website. Copies of this book are available through CareNet programs and links on my website, below.

CareNet of North Carolina
http://www.carenetinc.org
CareNet of North Carolina
2000 W. First Street, Suite 410
Winston-Salem, NC 27104

Anam Cara
Collegial Clergy Communities
by Mahan Siler
© Copyright 2009, Mahan Siler
ISBN 13: 978-0-9767450-2-0
ISBN 10: 0-9767450-2-X
Library of Congress Control Number: 2009934425
All rights reserved
Updated Edition, 2009

To order, or for more information, please contact:
http://www.mahansiler.com
info@mahansiler.com

Design & Publishing Services by Publications Unltd • Raleigh, North Carolina
WWW.PUBLICATIONSUNLTD.COM

Dedication

To the chutzpa of pastors.

The courage, week after week, to declare the gracious reality of God with words that fall short every time,

the courage to stand with conviction, offering an alternative worldview of Shalom to the dominant culture of competitive, often violent ways of relating,

the courage to enter, upon invitation, into the private places of a person's life and be there with presence, faith and sometimes sight,

the courage to call for surrender to the Christ Spirit that takes us often where we do not wish to go,

the courage to be a flawed leader of an imperfect institution that frequently contradicts the compassion it espouses,

and the courage to bear the symbols of God, even be a symbol of God, at the perilous risk of playing God.

The mission of CareNet of North Carolina, a wholly owned subsidiary of North Carolina Baptist Hospital, is to "combine the wisdom from faith traditions and the behavioral sciences to heal the mind, body, spirit, and community." This holistic approach to care is central to the faith communities understanding of healing and is shared by the medical center of which we are connected.

Our professional ministry of faith-integrated counseling, prevention and wellness education, consultation, and coaching that enhances mental and spiritual health are services we provide to communities where we have ministry locations. All of these services share the hope of creating healthier and stronger communities.

One such community that we have strong ties is the faith community. We serve as a major referral source for clergy who have parishioners needing specialized mental health care. Many of these clergy are isolated and lonely and regularly seek our centers for care and consultation.

AnamCara is a way of practicing pastoral ministry that invites relationship, supports accountability, and provides a safe place to share in a collegial community. This vision is very compatible with our mission at CareNet of developing collegial and collaborative relationships with those committed to the health of clergy and communities.

I am pleased to reconnect on the trail with Dr. Mahan Siler who has been hiking along the path of pastoral ministry for over fifty years. His vision for AnamCara as a holistic way for clergy to walk together in a collegial community will extend our care to clergy in a new and imaginative way. As Mahan states in the pages that follow, "AnamCara is a radical alternative to our culture's pervasive individualism, an embodiment of life with God in community."

I am grateful for the opportunity that CareNet can partner with a vision for ministry that is rooted in generative friendships that share the practice of ministry through honest dialogue, theological reflection and discernment, leadership, and Spirit awareness.

Steven N. Scoggin, Psy.D, LPC
President, CareNet, Inc.

Contents

Acknowledgements   xi

Preface
    The Wager   1
    What if?   3
    Genesis of AnamCara   4

AnamCara: Collegial Clergy Communities
    What Is AnamCara?   7
    For Whom Are AnamCara Communities?   8
    AnamCara as Jam Session   9
    Common Praxis   11
       Practicing Community   11
       Practicing Theological Reflection and Discernment   14
       Practicing Leadership   16
       Practicing Soul Nurturance   20
    Integration of Practicing   24
    Invitation: Setting the Table   25
    Notes and Resources   26

Appendix I
    Response to Questions   31

Appendix II
    Covenant   35

Appendix III
    Designing the Time   37

Appendix IV
    A Model of Case Presentation   39

Acknowledgements

This is a thank offering. My vision of AnamCara, a way of practicing pastoral ministry, is an expression of my gratitude for our vocation. More often than not, our vocation has kept me under its spell since that revelatory moment in a seminary class when, in response to the professor's unpacking a pastoral dilemma, I whispered, "I want to do that!" And I have, for over fifty years.

As a veteran in our craft, I have trekked enough switchbacks on our trail to reach a plateau with a vista. From that place I can look back, watching others of you make your way. What strikes me is this: most of you are walking alone. There are exceptions. I also see a few clusters of you hiking together, and I imagine you engaging in playful bantering and serious exchanges in between interludes of extended silence.

This thank offering is a particular way of walking together. And it is the product of numerous conversations with those whom I have met along the trail and who have joined me in playful bantering and serious exchanges about our vocation.

This includes CareNet of North Carolina. CareNet, a network of faith-integrated counseling, education, consultation and coaching, has adopted AnamCara as an extension of its mission. CareNet both facilitates AnamCara groups and trains facilitators of AnamCara communities.

I am also thinking of the over thirty clergy who have participated in the four clergy groups from 2001–2007. The first of these clergy groups was funded by grants from The Louisville Institute. In addition, editor Ulrike Guthrie has once again helped me with style and structure. Carol Majors has shepherded the publication of this revision.

To each one I am grateful.

Mahan Siler, July 2009

Preface

This I have in common with you who are ministers of congregations:[1] we have bet our vocational life on a reality we cannot see or measure or control. When I step back, I find this risk astounding. At some point, and many times since, you too were drawn into and felt embraced by gracious Mystery whose essence is nothing less than unconditional Love, unrelenting Justice. That Mystery, most clear and compelling in Jesus, desires incarnation in the world, Spirit from which no-thing in life or death, now or later, can separate us. You wagered that there is a God like Abba, *mysterium tremendum et fascinans:*[2] holy *mystery* that makes us *tremble,* takes our breath away, yet lures us with *fascination.*

So strong was this embrace and mutual longing that you staked your vocational life on the wild, generous Spirit that wishes to live through you. Daily you gamble with what you have, your life energy. Daily you place your bet with the coins of your time—50, 60, 70 hours a week; 50, 60, 70 years of life—declaring a wager that can look foolish in our post enlightenment world that distrusts what cannot be rationally explained. You engage this Presence. You doubt. You adore. You wonder. You stammer. But this fact remains: without the existence of this transcendent Spirit our vocation collapses into folly.

You would have other words to express your calling but words no less bold, mysterious, and faltering. You didn't choose this vocation for its prudence, lucrative possibilities, or status. With a mixture of knowing and not-knowing, you and I said "yes," a full bodied "yes." We said "yes" and we say it still.

In time this calling to love God and the "other" as yourself led you to pastoral leadership of a congregation.[3] Abruptly your nose pressed against the glass of a paradox: spirit always seeks expression in form, like churches; yet these same institutional forms can stifle the spirit that birthed them.

The natural tendency of any institution, including the church, is toward certainty, pride, survival, security, familiarity—not toward mystery, adventure, humility, surrender. Most of us were ill prepared to encounter this gravitational pull that can undermine risk, deny failure, seek control, lose memory, and domesticate mystery.

In your institutional role, daily you live the tension of being both leader and manager; facing the world as prophet, facing the congregation as pastor; feeling the pull of mission, feeling the press of maintenance; affirming self-worth, summoning self-sacrifice; creating discomfort, reducing discomfort; communicating with poetry in worship, communicating with prose in e-mails; both called by God and employed for paid services. In living these ongoing contradictions, the power of the congregational system rightfully challenges you to focus your calling in concrete ways. But this power, if excessive, will douse the "bush" fire that became a "fire in your belly." The fire that fueled your wager can grow dim and flicker.

Furthermore, you lead an institution in a time of broad distrust of institutions. The mantra these days, "I am spiritual but not religious," translated means, "I want self-transcending experiences of the sacred but I am 'turned off,' even repelled by religious institutions." And strangely, for some persons the more they engage Jesus, the more disillusioned, even embarrassed, they feel about the church that bears his name. You, as well, wince over the same words of faith, life-giving to you, that are used in life-denying ways by others. You have devoted yourself to an institution suffering from multiple personalities, waning respect, and even hostility.[4]

How do you stoke the fire of soul within your institutional role? How do you keep alive your curiosity about this mysterious generosity that wants to surge through you and your ministry? How do you lead with passion and vision within a congregation that may desire more management than leadership, more comfort than challenge, more efficiency than effectiveness?

My response, from fifty years in our vocation, is this: You cannot by yourself. Without soul friends, vital pastoral leadership is not possible. A single log will not long remain aflame.

You know this truth. You have been formed and reformed by the generosity of friends. Mentors, teachers, seminary classmates, lay members, colleagues, and "just friends" along the way have connected

AnamCara—Collegial Clergy Communities

with you at the deep level of soul—embodying grace, sharing wisdom, igniting laughter, nourishing spirit, cherishing stories.

But I am suggesting something more radical. I'm advocating a circle of soul friends who share your vocation. In that circle you practice intentionally what you practice mostly on your own. I am raising the question: what if you, with a few collegial friends, regularly practice together being in community, nourishing soul, reflecting theologically, and mutually consulting on each other's leadership? What if in your gathering together you formed a holding place through support, collaboration, and accountability? What if you shift your center of gravity from doing ministry solo to offering ministry from within a peer community of friends? This booklet unpacks this query: *What if?*

Communities of common praxis are not new. Indeed, they join a lively tradition. In other times of social and religious upheaval, intentional communities have sprung up to provide sacred spaces for worship, learning, reflection, friendship, accountability, and service to the world. Think of the religious orders of the Roman Catholic tradition, the Beguines of the medieval period, Spener's cell groups in the seventeenth-century Lutheran church, Wesleyan small groups in the eighteenth century, and within the twentieth century the Iona Community begun in Scotland and the Oxford Movement birthing the network of Twelve-Step Recovery Groups. All of these examples share this conviction in *the transforming power of small, caring communities formed around spiritual practices with support and accountability.* My vision of clergy communities responds to the same impulse.

Much is in the air these days about the value of spiritual practices and small groups of clergy friends. We have been seeing this shift toward peer learning communities in recent years. Clinical Pastoral Education has embodied an alternative model to solo ministry with its small collegial communities of collaboration and accountability under the supervision of a skilled facilitator. Doctor of Ministry programs place mutual learning with clergy colleagues at their core. The Shalem Institute supports clergy groups addressing the interface between the contemplative life and leadership. Parker Palmer's "circles of trust,"[5] originally designed for teachers, are now being extended to clergy. And recently, Lilly Endowment Inc. has invested over eighty million dollars through grants for programs in Sustaining Pastoral

Excellence, many of which have incorporated small peer communities for learning and support.[6]

However, many of these seminars or groups are "add ons" to an already full schedule, not a reorientation of ministry itself. Some of the current clergy groups focus more on insight and understanding than on transformative practices. Others concentrate on one or two practices, not the integration of multiple disciplines. Also they are temporary. Educational opportunities, like Clinical Pastoral Education and Doctor of Ministry programs, do provide alternative ways to experience pastoral leadership, that is, within a practicing community of peers. But after the educational experience is completed, most participants return to a solo model. Like rubber bands, these small peer groups stretch to this new way of being in ministry, but once the provided structure is released, most pastors return to an overly individualized way of ministry. The model of lone leader is familiar and well established. It's the norm. The ruts are deep. The wheels on our vocational vehicle turn unbidden in that direction.[7] Ministry remains essentially an individual affair.

This is the dominant defining narrative of our vocation: We fly solo. We are on our own to give shape to our work. It is up to us to interpret the gospel, read the "signs" of our time in history, intuit feedback, determine our use of time, judge appropriate responses to congregational crises, face into conflict, establish practices of self-care, worship while leading in worship, and integrate the learning from the plethora of resources available to us. Autonomy and individualism are the fatal flaws of our vocation.

I'm advocating a different narrative, a contrast to flying solo. We can fly in community, something like geese in formation. Flying, for geese, requires less energy because of shared leadership and mutual sensitivities. Similarly, I see a small circle of soul friends who meet regularly to practice together the essentials of our vocation, namely, theological reflection and discernment, leadership and spirituality.

The Genesis of AnamCara

In 1983, I moved from being a director of a department of pastoral care in a medical center to serving as pastor of Pullen Memorial Baptist Church in Raleigh, North Carolina.[8] The contrast in my

AnamCara — Collegial Clergy Communities

roles as leader was striking. In my new pastoral role, there were few measures of accountability. At first I reveled in the freedom to shape my ministry on my own. But soon my sense of freedom gave way to the constriction of unspoken agreements and unnamed expectations. Beneath the burden of freedom, I felt alone in my scramble to define my role as leader.

I joined a circle of friends, a small group of men with now thirty years of life together. We gifted each other with an acceptance close to unconditional. We were bound by commitments to each other, including our presence two hours every two weeks, plus two extended retreats twice a year. It was the container I needed. With these friends, I found support for my life — but less so for my life as pastor.

I needed more. I wanted to be with pastors who could focus with me on our efforts at priestly and prophetic faithfulness. I began to look for peers with whom I could be out of role, yet peers who experienced the role daily. Before long, I sent out an invitation to a circle of clergy friends to participate in what I called Sabbath Day:

"I fear we have internalized the hallmark of our American culture — individualism. For all our talk about communion and indeed for all our efforts in building community with others, we tend to craft our work by ourselves. What Alexis de Tocqueville said of our forbears in Democracy in America could be said of us: 'They form the habit of thinking of themselves in isolation and imagine that their whole destiny is in their hands.'

Instead of continuing this way, I wonder if you would be interested in being part of a clergy Sabbath Day — a time to nurture our souls with colleague-friends who put a face to the grace in Christ, a time to return to our first love, God, a time to be reminded that the ministry of the church belongs to God and not to us."

Three pastors responded. Each Wednesday for several years we set aside a Sabbath day for silence, prayer, conversation, rest, and walking in the woods. Yet over time, the full day became a half-day, then an occasional half-day, and finally no day at all. Our clergy Sabbaths, like sand castles, gave way to wave after wave of pressing congregational needs. This fragile container of sacred space cracked, then crumbled.

Absent was a commitment as strong as the other scheduled commitments of the week. We were unable to maintain the container in which we addressed our basic needs: a safe place for voicing personal and vocational concerns, discussing leadership issues with those who shared our same work, returning to our Source of calling through silence and word, pondering the role of the church in our current cultural context, and through it all, enjoying friendship with stories, laughter, ritual, and mutual care. Missing was a strong trellis,[9] a stable structure to hold up the growing vines of our lives.

During these last ten years in retirement, I have tested my awareness and intuitions as pastor by organizing and co-leading four ecumenical clergy groups, each of eight to ten participants, who have met regularly for either a year or eighteen months. In addition, I have served as a consultant to a Lilly-funded project of two clergy peer groups that met for two years. Also, I draw insight from two clergy groups in the Washington D.C. area who were started by two pastors who participated in the first cycle of AnamCara communities. As of this writing, one of these groups in entering into their second year and the other group is entering its fifth year together.

My underlying question in forming these collegial groups was this: Will these clergy leaders of congregations complete their lengthy commitment saying, "This has been another good continuing education experience, thank you very much." Or will they say, "*This being in collegial community is a primary context from which I want to offer ministry*"? In other words, will they regard the experience as an educational "add on" or will they see and embrace another way of being in ministry? Their responses have encouraged this next step of refinement and broader exposure.

Thus, from my pastoral experience and my learning from clergy participants, I have formed a vision of communities of generative friendships among ministers who gather regularly to practice the art of theological reflection and discernment, leadership and Spirit awareness in their life and ministry. I lift up and offer to you this particular way of leading congregations from within intentional community.

AnamCara:
Collegial Clergy Communities

I can no longer imagine doing pastoral ministry without my group of soul friends. Our time together often feels like a taste of the Kingdom, a feast of deep laughter and friendship among competent peers who respect each other. In a wonderfully paradoxical way, the worship, study, and conversation we share make a better pastor and remind me there is more to my life than ministry.

—Steve Hyde, participant of an AnamCara circle entering its fifth year[10]

What Is AnamCara?[11]

AnamCara redefines ministry. It embodies a shift from seeing ourselves working solo to identifying ourselves as pastors in a peer community. Vocationally, "I" becomes "we." It is a radical alternative to our culture's pervasive individualism. Within a small circle of colleagues, we learn and acknowledge, "Without you, I cannot be the minister I want to be; without me, you cannot be the minister you want to be."

As Joyce wrote, "Our days together turned out not to be a 'break' from the demands and challenges we faced daily, but the very foundation for responding to our various calls with fresh insight and renewed strength, gleaned from drinking together at the well of faith."

AnamCara is a network of small collegial circles of five to eight clergy leaders[12] of congregations who meet regularly to offer mutual support, collaboration, and accountability in their practices of theological reflection and discernment, leadership and soul care.[13] So that these clergy can be free from their accustomed leadership roles, a skilled facilitator of process will guide the flow of the one full day a month gathering. In addition, along with intercessory prayer, AnamCara participants will connect informally each week, either face-to-face over coffee or a meal, by telephone, or over the internet. Beginning with a retreat, each AnamCara group clarifies its covenant together for a year. At the end of the year, AnamCara groups in a retreat setting take time to evaluate and celebrate along with the opportunity to terminate or renew their covenant.

More simply, this is about friends, soul friends, friends with whom we share the passion of common calling. In the Celtic tradition, a person who acted as teacher, companion, and spiritual guide was called an *anam cara* (soul friend).[14] With the *anam cara* you could share your intimate self, telling the stories of your life. Stories, we know from experience, both require community and create community. We know as well that for the soul to show up there must be sufficient safety.[15] AnamCara would be a small circle of your choosing, friends of your excitements, companions you could risk trusting, colleagues with whom you would enjoy practicing the art of ministry.

AnamCara is not another event of continuing education, nor a study, support, therapy, prayer, or lectionary group. AnamCara is not just a way-station for nourishment, a break from the marathon run that ministry can be, a practicum for leadership, or a place to sharpen the skill-set for ministry. These are secondary gains.

AnamCara communities are practice groups. Practicing, not mutual belief, is the unifying thread. The common praxis—being in community, theological reflection and discernment, leading, and soul nurturance—provides the trellis. Or to call on another metaphor, these four basic practices provide the skeleton. Each group will flesh out these practices in its own way.

For Whom Are AnamCara Communities?

AnamCara is for you who are "grassroots" theologians, leaders of local faith-communities, and Spirit-persons yet readily *confess* that you cannot practice theological reflection, leadership, or spiritual awareness by yourselves or under your own strength. It is for you who want to *profess* more intentionally a practice of ministry that challenges the individualism that isolates us, seduces us with self-importance, and insulates us from the resources of interdependence.

I am addressing those of you with longings sufficiently strong to consider re-structuring the way you offer ministry with congregations.

- Weary from the isolation and fatigue of attempting an overly privatized ministry, you may be drawn to the possibility of a community in which you would be out of role with peers who understand the role.
- Leading in the midst of theological ferment where people struggle, both consciously and unconsciously, with the fundamental questions of faith, you might value a setting with vocational friends who share the same striving for theological clarity and discernment.
- Overseeing a complex congregational system, as both priest and prophet,[16] you may long for a balcony, a place apart with colleagues that offers emotional distance for the perspective, imagination, and centeredness that leadership requires.
- Knowing the risk of losing your soul within the role, you might welcome a place apart with colleagues where you can regularly recover the Source of your calling and reclaim your core identity in God's grace, not in work.

AnamCara as Jam Session

Allow a story, turned metaphor, to convey the tone and substance of what I envision.

We were wrapping up another banjo lesson. Cary Fridley, my teacher, began describing the work involved in "cutting" her next CD: recruiting musicians, practicing privately, practicing together again and again—all in preparation for the final recording session.

"I get increasingly anxious as we approach the recording," she admitted. "Well," I asked, "what helps you with your anxiety?" Her response was profound beyond her knowing. "When I can get to that place with myself and with others where the music is more important than me, then I am not anxious."

In our work, we become the focus of projections and expectations, all of which can ratchet up our performance anxiety. Furthermore, in the eyes of many, we are paid to be the primary carriers of the church's anxiety. As with Cary, the static of anxious self-preoccupation, from whatever source, will undermine our inner freedom to yield to the Music.

How do we get to that that place where the Music of the gospel becomes again and again more important than we are? With friends, I submit. I imagine pastors circling up with other colleagues to "jam,"[17] to lose and find themselves again in the Music. I picture AnamCara as one of those gathering places where vocational friends practice, improvise, harmonize, note the discordant sounds, learn from one another, laugh with one another over mistakes—in other words, to love the Music together.

Of course, there is the need to practice privately. But to jam with others adds another layer to learning and to the likelihood of joy. This kind of practicing is more heart work than hard work. We take the time to play with ideas and possibilities without the pressure of deadlines. Then returning from the jam to the swirling vortex of performing ministry, the Music will more likely sustain us and be heard by congregants as well.

The concept of *liminality*[18] from cultural anthropology is another way to picture the intent of AnamCara. With a few colleagues we step off the conveyor belt of ordinary work and cross over a threshold (*limen*) into an extra-ordinary open, receptive place. We intentionally leave behind the press of things to do and enter into a clear space with curiosity about the new that might happen. It is a holding place with friends. This space invites transformation by our stepping back, clarifying, and deepening our calling before re-crossing the threshold (*limen*), returning to the work that awaits us.

In ministry, especially in worship and pastoral care, we deliberately create these safe, expectant, *liminal spaces* that invite the possibility of transformation. It is critical to have these places for ourselves. AnamCara would be such a place.

Common Praxis

Let's return to the four basic practices, noted above, that require further elaboration.

Each AnamCara community addresses four questions:

1. How will we practice being in community?
2. How will we practice reflecting upon and discerning the movement of God in our lives, in the life of the congregation and in the life of our times?
3. How will we collaborate around each person's practice of leadership?
4. How will we practice prayer and worship in ways that re-open us to the transforming power of the gospel, both individually and as a circle of friends?

Practicing Community

> *"I see myself in a deep hole, by myself, digging away furiously. Then I look up and see members gathering around the lip of the hole cheering me on."*
> —AnamCara participant

I am not the first to lament the isolation of pastors. I join the chorus of observers of clergy who ask: Why is pastoral ministry mostly offered by individuals in virtual isolation? Isolation in our vocation can be acute.[19]

Aloneness is built into our vocation; it is inescapable and persistent. But isolation is not. I draw a distinction between aloneness and isolation. Aloneness, being set apart, comes with our job. It is inherent, a given. Isolation, however, is being cut off from significant relationships. Isolation starves our spirit.

In the above quotation, my pastor friend was experiencing isolation, seeing himself in a hole becoming deeper with each stroke, all the while being cheered on for his hard work by approving congregants. At that time, absent for him were friendships rooted in mutual care. His challenge, and ours, is how to accept and even embrace the aloneness while overcoming the isolation.

I see three primary sources that contribute to the aloneness inherent in our vocation.

First, the clergy *role* brings with it a particular kind of aloneness. It accompanies the robe we don, the Bible we lift in worship, the collar we wear. As pastoral leaders of congregations, we are both *human beings* and *living symbols of more than we are.*[20] Both are true and remain in tension. While in every sense "just human beings," we are not "one of the gang," like everybody else. We are walking, talking, embodied representatives of more than ourselves. We are signs pointing beyond ourselves to the larger Reality we name God. Our vocational life is a wager that God is real, a divine presence in whom "we live and move and have our being." And this symbolic identity deepens with each passing pastoral visit, funeral, wedding, and worship service.

More than a symbol, we are to be symbolic exemplars.[21] As the ordination of Episcopal clergy words it, we vow to be "wholesome examples" of the gospel. Many leaders in other fields are symbols of more than they are, but few leaders carry such additional moral pressure. Pastors, and in some sense their families, are expected to show, as well as tell, what loving God and neighbor looks like.

This authority from our symbolic role is both a dangerous burden to carry and life-giving power that can name, bless, and heal. We experience both, feeling deeply the weight and the privilege of this power. Deliberately, and with realism, the ordination sets us apart as different — not more important, but different. This aloneness that companions our role is the unwritten, usually misunderstood, portion of our work. It comes with the job.

Note a second source of aloneness. Ministers experience an unusual work arrangement. You are employed, remunerated by, and accountable to employers with a limited grasp of your job. How could it be otherwise with most of your ministry invisible, much of it private and confidential, and expectations more unconscious than conscious? Even those closest to us cannot grasp the contours of our work. Have you not felt defensive and inadequate when trying to explain exactly the work you do? Job descriptions fall short every time. This partial knowledge of a pastor's work is inevitable, a condition possibly modified but never eliminated. It's hard not to feel out of focus, thus lonely, in the midst of unacknowledged assumptions and limited understanding.

In many pastors I sense a third source of aloneness. We may experience pressure to preach or teach what counters our own beliefs. Or, we may avoid going public with a deeply held personal conviction. In such moments, we feel out of sync with the prevailing beliefs in our congregation or denomination, especially if the valuing of differences is not present in key relationships. This tension between public and private selves is not only another source of loneliness. It can be debilitating to our spirit.

As a way to overcome loneliness in our work, all of us turn to our families and close friends in the congregation for support. The danger comes in asking for more. When we ask for counsel, our close relationships will compromise the objectivity and distance that consultation requires. Besides, expecting vocational counsel from either family or church friends places on them a burden not theirs to carry. Soul friends, however, who know this role from the inside out, offer a rich source for vocational understanding.[22]

While aloneness companions us, we need not remain in isolation. AnamCara is one antidote to isolation. This is its power: being in community out of the pastoral role with colleagues who know this role. And from this nurturing space we resource each other with support, collaboration, and accountability. We place ourselves within relationships where we are not alone in being alone.

Guy found it so. "Being part of a clergy peer community showed me a 'more excellent way' of living out my calling, a way which brought conversation and support into the isolated echo-chamber of ministry as I had most often practiced it."

If it is true that we live the tension of being both a human being and a symbol of more than we are, then AnamCara accentuates being human together. In contrast to the pressure of being "wholesome examples" of the gospel, AnamCara offers a place to let our guard down, allow immaturities to surface, acknowledge failure, mourn our loses, and permit potentials to be seen and affirmed. And knowing that we cannot fully join the very community we serve, AnamCara offers a life together without role restrictions.[23]

Amy made this very point. "As ministers we seek to try and provide this sense of community and family within the church. Collegial Community was an opportunity for me to experience that which I hope to provide for others."

Mahan Siler

Practicing Theological Reflection and Discernment

> *"I don't have time to think, I mean reflect theologically."*
> —pastor friend

This honest admission of my friend opens the way to our second practice. The discipline of theological reflection is difficult to develop and sustain amid the rush from appointment to appointment. And given our intellectual climate, even when there is the time, many of us are more comfortable reflecting psychologically or politically or sociologically. I am voicing the need for theological leadership.

In fact, we are resident theologians, reflective practitioners. In contrast to academic theologians, we do theology more inductively, often starting with the daily struggles and joys of a particular people.[24] In theological reflection two practices are at work: thinking of ideas, calling upon metaphors, telling stories (often biblical) that illuminate meaning of life experiences. In tandem, discernment is the practice of intuiting with others where the Spirit might be in evidence. This theological reflection is both head and heart work.[25]

Intentional or not, in our preaching, teaching, administrating, and pastoral care we practice theological reflection and discernment day in and day out. We are on the frontlines helping people sort through the content and implications of faith as it relates to their lives in the world. This is costly, thought-provoking work especially when our thoughts and intuitions provoke dissonance.

I admire your willingness to join the battle over which narratives will define us. You and I keep telling the story of God over against other stories that vie to shape our identities. You consistently place the kingdom of God, a map of reality, alongside of other maps and join the fray knowing that the future belongs to the most accurate map, the most compelling story.

What a challenging period in history to be a pastoral theologian! The current social, political, religious, and economic upheavals are often depicted by contemporary seers as paradigm shifts, as profound transitions.[26] We serve in formidable times characterized by both blustery religiosity and relentless secularization. The shrill sounds of fundamentalists and atheists serve as bookends to the frequent religious vagueness in between. Yet within this whirlpool of secular doubts, religious and political ideologies, and religious vagueness, many people soulfully long to be a part of a larger narrative that grants meaning and promises roots. There seems to be a widespread discontent, restlessness, yearning for Something More, a hunger for the Sacred that is palpable today in a way not so evident earlier in my ministry. A trip to the religious or spirituality section of a bookstore bears witness to this change.

Even within your congregation there is a wide spectrum of theological perspectives. A consensus of central beliefs is unlikely. At one end, there are congregants who are comfortable with and nourished by traditional theological concepts. At the other end of the spectrum are members for whom the more conventional understandings of God, Jesus, and bible have lost traction. They are looking for fresh ways of interpreting and confessing their faith, ways that remain faithful to their tradition. In between these poles are members too preoccupied with other matters to reflect on their faith. They may be too frightened to probe their theological assumptions, and perhaps resent the challenge to do so.

As pastors, we work along the edges of this wide spectrum. Into the mix of worldviews we keep dropping pinches of yeast for theological fermentation. During pastoral rounds, we raise theological questions, provide theological framing of issues, and express our own theological convictions, while at the same time trying to honor differences. It's a high wire act requiring careful balancing.

Some pastors are accused of failure of nerve, of not being willing to speak up and out on critical issues of our time. Their caution, where it is accurate, may come more from *lack of clarity* than *lack of courage*. It takes energy and time to discern your sense of the Spirit in complex social and ethical dilemmas. When we can become clear and therefore decisive, most of us are willing to take stands even if costly. Plus, it's our clarity that frees us to listen to other voices without defensiveness. But where and with whom do we search for such clarity?

I am raising the option of space in your calendars and a place with other pastoral theologians to step back and reflect on the gospel we are declaring. From that space we can ask with peers: Where is the Spirit active within our congregation (including ourselves) and where does the Spirit seem to be leading the larger church in our moment in history? In that place we can probe with other pastoral thinkers how to speak of faith in our situation. Without this priority, we are prone to theological sound bites quickly worded in the rush of ministry, or we run the risk of depending too much on the theological thinking of others.

The resource of colleagues within a learning community such as AnamCara is just such a place in which to ponder the big questions, enter into deep listening, and think critically about the vision that keeps calling us.

Practicing Leadership

> *"My leadership has two faces: I am a hospice chaplain to those members grieving the loss of what was; I am a midwife, helping the birthing of new life among us."*
> —AnamCara participant

This pastor reflects the challenge of leadership: leading amid the loss of what was and the excitement of what can be. He sees himself standing in the breach, honoring both his grief ministry and midwife role.

But note, this pastor sees himself as a leader. Frankly, it took me a while to regard myself as leader of leaders within a congregational system. Without difficulty I understood that I was preacher, liturgist, teacher, administrator, deliverer of pastoral care, and participant in the life of the larger community. Only with time did I see these as ways I expressed leadership.

Today you don't have my luxury of gradually coming to this awareness. You are leaders. The times demand it. Every institution, it seems, clamors for effective leaders of change.

Or do they clamor for effective management? There is a difference. Managers ask: "Are we doing things right?" Leaders ask: "Are we doing the right things?"[27] The church, as every institution, requires both—managers and leaders. I am guessing you feel the pressure to be both.

As managers we work toward efficiency, security, and consistency. There is a "right" way to function. Problems can be named, defined through discussion, and then implemented through action. When managing, we are present oriented, seeking ways to reduce anxiety, provide reasonable policies, and monitor follow-through actions.

As leaders we ask different questions: Who are we? What is our purpose? What has God called us to be and to do? Who is our neighbor?

We gather the congregation around the right questions that defy rapid, problem-solving answers. When leading we are future and direction oriented, often causing discomfort with our provocative questions about identity and mission. At such times we create anxiety in the service of moving from known realities into unknown possibilities.

You are both leader and a manager of a family of faith and a complex institution. While these roles are shared with others who lead and manage with you, you are the "overseer." Your position in the congregational system is critical for influencing its direction. From experience we know that unless there is reasonably good management ("are we doing things right?") leadership will not be taken seriously. And we know that without leadership ("are we doing the right things?") church becomes self-absorbed, an end in itself.

Your challenge to lead is huge. We are offering leadership amid multiple cultural and religious transitions,[28] some of which we have noted. The rate of change, perhaps the central fact of our time, comes not arithmetically, 2–4–6–8, but exponentially, 2–4–8–16–32. Our historical moment is bathed in chronic anxiety. According to family systems' theorist Ed Friedman,[29] our society functions like a chronically anxious, regressed family, marked by high reactivity, blaming the other, herding into polarized camps, and insisting on quick-fix solutions. This high anxiety courses like an electrical current through all institutions, including the church.

But leadership calls for opposite behaviors. In contrast to the four anxious behaviors, effective leadership summons:

reasoned responses, not reactivity
taking *responsibility,* not blaming
collaboration and *dialogue,* not herding into groups; and
long-term solutions, not quick-fixes.

No wonder daring leadership is so exceptional in our day.

Furthermore, we lead at a time when there is little consensus about what a congregation is for and therefore what a pastor is for. Amid such change and uncertainty, you try to discern what risks of innovation are needed to keep the church vibrant and what calming actions are needed to stabilize the congregation. You weigh constantly when to induce anxiety through challenge and when to reduce anxiety through calming presence. You walk the line with lay leaders seeking to know when to search for answers to defined problems and when to lean into the right questions. You finger this sharp edge: the challenge to know, define, and offer yourself in leading; and the danger of either promoting yourself or losing yourself in the needs and expectations of congregants.

I am left wondering where and with whom a pastor sorts out these challenges of leadership and management? With whom do we sort out these ambiguities? Isolated, it is impossible. I submit that with other clergy leaders clarity emerges, creativity surfaces, options appear, and stamina for next steps is given.

This was Nancy's experience. "Unlike so much of pastoral work, the reflective task cannot be done alone. The gravitational pulls to be a manager of programs and institutional needs are fierce. My experience with an AnamCara group enabled me discernment time, time to remember my true calling, and my unique work in the midst of many pulls."

Of course the needs of church members and institutional concerns influence us. Obviously they open possibilities for ministry. But when these pulls control our use of time, then our pastoral stance becomes reactive. We lose our equilibrium.

A reactive ministry forfeits a feature of our basic covenant with the congregation. In the ritual of ordination the church calls us to be pastoral leaders, saying in part, "Pastor, we set you apart. We will free you from making a living like the rest of us, so you can be free, not only to respond to our immediate needs, but also to step back and ponder how the Story intersects with our stories, both individually and collectively. We liberate you to bring to us a different perspective that is placed alongside of our understanding. Together, from different angles, we have our best chance of claiming our life together in mission."[30]

This sounds idealistic because it is counter-intuitive for the congregation as well. Most congregants want direct service. They may be mirroring the force they feel at their work; namely, immediate action, measurable results. The pressure to survive and thrive can blind all of us to the invisible, less obvious need for the leader to stand apart in order to see from a difference perspective. From that place of disengagement, along with engagement, the pastor is better able to offer, "This is my sense of God's movement among us . . . what do you see?"

Congregational life resembles the frenzy on a dance floor. Members are dancing in twos, threes, sometimes ballroom dancing, waltzing, even line dancing, sometimes solo dancing, and seldom to the same tune. As pastors we move in and out of these dances, often feeling out of place, frequently confused about next steps. To be able to dance well and with delight, we must periodically get to the balcony and catch our breath (Spirit). From the balcony we can look for patterns, see where we have been dancing and note where we might reenter the dance. The whirling energy of the dance floor will eventually exhaust and overwhelm us. The balcony provides respite and detached attentiveness.[31]

Many helping professionals like physicians and psychotherapists turn to colleagues for consultation. In contrast, collaboration with other pastors about leadership rarely happens. When confronting critical situations in the congregation, we are unlikely to access the wisdom of other pastors. Yet, who better to offer collaboration than those who share with us the same craft? Colleagues, I believe, can be available, not to analyze or fix, but to listen and ask clarifying questions within a circle of mutual respect. AnamCara meets on the "balcony."

In liminal space with a small group of peers, we can review our leadership in two ways: support the on-going inner work of defining one's direction in ministry; and, through case presentations, reflect on our specific ways of leading.[32] (See Appendix IV for an example of the process of case presentation.) Left alone, we risk losing our footing amid the anxious reactivity that characterizes our time and often the life of our congregations.

Practicing Soul Nurturance

> *"The more I speak of God the less I seem to encounter the reality of God."*
> —AnamCara participant

The most serious danger I faced as pastor was losing my soul in fulfilling the role.[33] It is a strange, disarming truth: in pointing regularly to God, we can lose the reality of God; in proclaiming Jesus, we can cease to hear his voice in our lives; while inviting others to catch the wind of the Spirit, our sails can remain furled.

Soul is that place of alignment with God's passion for mercy and justice, a stance of wide openness to Grace at our core, a center where our being and divine being connect. Soul awareness is remembering our first love, both the priority of loving God with all we are and loving because God first loved us.[34] The soul is the furnace from which refining flame, light, and energy arises into our ministry. I place this practice last, not because it is least important, but because without Fire the other practices of being in community, theological reflection, and pastoral leadership cannot be maintained.

During my first [solo] flight as full-time pastor, I flew high and long, with few stops for soul care. My energy, stored from years of preparation, seemed endless. Eventually, spiritual and emotional fatigue set in, then bewilderment, and finally disillusionment. The self-giving required in ministry eventually exhausted the very love that gave birth to it.[35] A casualty from combining unrealistic ideals for self and church, I resigned with no ministry in sight, wondering if I was resigning my vocation as well. So I know this poignancy, losing touch with the very Source of life that summons us to vocation and sustains us along the way.[36] In my case, years later, I was given a graceful second chance to attempt our role with soul.

Being a self with soul or being a person within Soul requires living a paradox. The apostle Paul can help us here. In Galatians, he names the seeming contradiction: "I, but not I, Christ living within [and through] me."[37] Certainly, Paul was an "I," a vivid personality with traits, flaws and gifts. Not timid. A strong ego, we can say. Yet, we listen to him because through his boldness we connect with Spirit, Love, living Christ. Both are critical, a strong sense of I or self and the surrender of self as vessel of the Christ life.

It takes a hearty ego, a solid self to make it in ministry: to hand-wrestle a biblical text before a congregation each week; to be able to challenge, as well as comfort the very people who pay our salary; to have our humanity on display; to be the object of evaluations we seldom hear; to be a Rorschach for outrageous projections; to hold confidential information without it showing.

Or the opposite—a diminished self or weak ego—will undermine the effectiveness of our work. Without a high degree of self-awareness, we run the risk of using ministry to meet our emotional needs. Indeed the more hard-earned self-knowledge we possess the less likely we are to project onto others our insecurities and past wounds. Rather than bypassing this inner exploration, soul nurturance includes a curiosity of knowing and valuing our unique selves.[38] We require sufficient self-worth to allow reasoned responses, not automatic reactions, to other people's behavior.

Yet even a healthy ego, as important a goal as that is, can keep *us* at the center. This we know from experience, a strong sense of self will resist the posture of servant, much preferring the ego need to be master with the illusion of control.[39] This is the human dilemma. But this dilemma intensifies in a vocation that thrusts us center stage.

I named earlier my transition from being a director of a hospital department to becoming senior pastor of an urban congregation. In the medical center I was responsible for one of many departments, a player on a large team. In returning to the pastorate I experienced an abrupt contrast. Suddenly I felt at the center, very public and prominent. Oddly, serving the church in the name of God appeared to have my name all over it. The seduction was fierce. My work seemed about me, my sermons, my pastoral care, my leadership. From adulation to censure, excessive attention came my way. Then I noticed the turned-up volume of inner voices saying, "You are not measuring up. You are not enough. Try harder." Or, "You are doing great. Keep it up." This interplay of inner and outer forces drew the conclusion—ministry is about me.

But, I hasten to add, our vocation also reminds us that ministry is not about us. Our work periodically wakes us up from the revelry of self-importance. Occasionally the sermon preaches us when self-consciousness steps aside and we sense ourselves a part of a spirited message beyond our creation. Or, when in those moments of stunned silence in the midst of a crisis we are somehow given the gift of calming presence and appropriate word. Or, there is the joy when someone "gets it"—that she is radically loved and cherished in spite of, that he is fully forgiven by God regardless. Or, when we stumble and fall, broken open to the same love in spite of and forgiveness regardless. And there are those holy times when, as midwives, we assist in the birth of new life in a person, family, congregation, or even larger community.

Yes, we can count on it, that in the daily round of daily pastoral duties, we come across those grace-full events from which we walk away saying, "Something was happening there that I cannot explain except with words like Spirit or God." And you whisper under your breath, "This is why I said 'yes' to this work!" In those moments we regain the soul truth, namely, that ministry at its depth is not about us. It is about this Christ Mystery living in, through and around us. It's about the Music, the Fire. Thank God, these moments in ministry come knocking at our door, leaving bread. As a friend of mine likes to say, our vocation is for our conversion.

The soul question then is one of identity:[40] "Who am I at the core?" What we preach and teach we can lose sight of for ourselves, namely that our little ego is only a small part of all that we are. We are part of bigger life, the "not I, but Christ living in us." Or as Jesus put it, we lose this smaller self at our center in order to find our center within the life of God. Our deepest identity comes from awakening to what we already are, the beloved of God. As obvious as we clergy can make it sound, few of us know—and keep remembering—that we are profoundly loved without conditions or limits.

So we can say, we have a ministry, but we are not our ministry. Ministry experiences, pleasant and not so pleasant, come and go, but they are not the source of our well-being or primary identity. Soul work strips away the thick defenses around our protective egos, pulling us inward and down to that place of yielding, letting go, and trusting the grace given, never achieved. AnamCara is a place with others to practice what we know to be true but have not fully internalized. We practice again and again returning to that Grace that doesn't change even though the life that carries us is constantly changing.

Or to recall the metaphor of the jam session, ego represents the role of the banjo and banjo player. We work hard to learn the skills of playing the instrument, that is, the craft of ministry. But the instrument and instrumentalist, however valued and accomplished, are nothing without the music. They exist for the music. Being visible, the banjo player with banjo draws our attention. But in the fullest sense, it is about the music, the Soul Music reverberating through the player, and doing so even more powerfully when played with others.

So if soul is at the center of our role, then who will ask us the questions such as: How is it with your soul? What helps you re-center, again and again, in God's grace? What practices take you beyond the egoic thinking of ordinary awareness to the deeper level of spiritual awareness? What reminds you who you really are? These are the questions of soul friends. AnamCara would be such a place and people.

Paula spoke about her experiences of spiritual practices in community. "The thing I valued most of this collegial clergy community was our time spent in lectio divina, prayer and silence together. All of these practices I do alone, but there is an energy and depth to these practices when done in community. And the depth is even greater when done in community where it is safe to be vulnerable."

In two ways AnamCara nurtures inner soul work. First, through common practices at every monthly gathering, each gathered group determines the specific spiritual practices. Examples of past AnamCara meetings have included lectio divina (praying the scripture), periods of solitude and silence, hymns and Taize chanting, Centering Prayer, and worship often incorporating the Eucharist. But this I found critical in designing the time together: maintain a balance between silence/solitude and words.

Second, each participant is given support and accountability around their personal spiritual practices. Of course, what nurtures the soul varies greatly among individuals in each circle. But AnamCara gives a place to discuss individual practices, exchange possibilities, report on their regular practicing in between meetings, and receive support for self-chosen disciplines.

Integration of Practicing

Practicing is the framework of this vision of AnamCara, for insight by itself is not transformative.[41] While insight opens options to us, it provides no energy or capacity for risking new behavior. As we have experienced in learning a language or a musical instrument, progress requires about 20% understanding and 80% practicing. And learning to speak a language or play a musical instrument is relational, requiring community. Only on-going practicing and more practicing, preferably with others, can deepen habits of the heart, mind, and action.[42]

See this vocational option as a rope consisting of these intertwining strands of practicing: forming communities of trust with a few colleagues; theological reflection/discernment, leadership, and nurturing soul. No one of these strands gives sufficient strength by itself. By itself, the practice of being in intimate community can degenerate into an unfocussed support group. By itself, theological reflection will encounter the limits of rational thinking. By itself, discernment may lack historical and biblical grounding. By itself, leading might accentuate process to the detriment of content and inner life. By themselves inner spiritual practices could by-pass the challenges of leadership and theological thinking. I propose an organic integration of these practices within a small circle of colleagues. AnamCara is a community of practitioners.

These interwoven strands of this rope are held together by support, collaboration, and accountability:

Support issues from the promise, "I commit myself to your growth as a person and minister; and I open myself to your commitment to my growth."

Collaboration accesses the understanding of colleagues who share the same calling both in giving and in receiving wisdom.

Accountability[43] provides the glue, reviewing honestly and gracefully the promises we have made, either as a group or as individuals.

Guy appreciated this benefit. "It was a gift . . . to know that there was a group of clergy friends who would ask about my growing-edges and hold me appropriately accountable for working on them."

AnamCara—Collegial Clergy Communities

Invitation: Setting the Table

In 1999 I attended a writing workshop led by novelist Peggy Payne. She challenged us to find an image that inspired, lured, and invited imagination. Magazines were strewn across the floor, full of possibilities. Two images, with words, leapt from the pages, begging, it seemed, for my attention. One, a picture of Stephen Spielberg with the caption: "Now you know." The other, a dining room scene entitled, "Setting the Table."

"Now I know," means, not "I know that this vision is valid," but rather, "I know this is what I see and want to make available." In those moments a shift occurred within me. This vision of collegial community, long in formation from my years as pastor, moved from being an idea of interest to becoming a summons to heed. I felt no wiggle room for procrastinating, only the imperative to give further shape to this vision and hurl it among other current efforts to sustain ministry.

"Setting the table" speaks to follow-through. I have described for you the menu of what you can expect if you come to the AnamCara table, a community of soul friends practicing together the Music by focusing on theological reflection/discernment, leadership collaboration, and soul nourishment.

I expect that this invitation to the table will appear daunting: another set of relationships to develop; another commitment of time to shoe-horn into your schedule; another emotional investment to make; and another layer of responsibility to assume. If so, you see accurately. The change would be substantial, not marginal.

Besides, some of you currently practice with colleagues. You are already finding collegiality in multiple ways, though not necessarily with the same friends. If my words confirm the strength you already receive from clergy friends present in your life, I am pleased.

For others, you might see more. This news of AnamCara could be good news. The pull to participate may be fervent enough to motivate a shift in your stance to ministry.[44] John Scherer notes that in order for significant change to be birthed, two "parents" must be present—pain and possibility.[45] Your discomfort may be sufficiently strong to risk a different way. And the possibility may be promising enough to support the realignments this would involve.

For you the table is set.

Mahan Siler

Notes and Resources

[1] By "ministers of congregations" I refer to ordained ministers who see themselves as pastoral leaders. They can include anyone on the ministerial staff of a church including pastor, associate pastor, minister of education, minister of music, etc. Also included are chaplains who are pastoral leaders within educational systems, the military, prisons, hospitals and retirement homes.

[2] Rudolf Otto's classic description of the experience of the sacred in *The Idea of the Holy* (Oxford: Oxford University Press, 1923).

[3] Your congregation may be a local church or a community within some other institution such as a prison or hospital.

[4] Leonard Sweet notes the shift from arguing *with* Christianity to arguing *against* Christianity. Examples are recent books on aggressive atheism written by Sam Harris, Richard Dawkins, David Dennett, and Frederick Crews. Sweet, editor, *The Perfect Storm* (Nashville, TN: Abingdon Press, 2008), pp. 19–20.

[5] See Parker J. Palmer, *A Hidden Wholeness* (San Francisco: Jossey-Bass, 2004).

[6] "Excellent ministry is collegial: It can only be done in the company of others in community," John Wimmer reported as a lesson learned from the Lilly-funded collective work on Sustaining Pastoral Excellence. From a presentation at the SPE forum, August 7, 2007, in Indianapolis, IN, published on the SPE website in an article entitled, "Key Lessons from SPE."

[7] Our vocation bears the marks of a Newtonian worldview that sees reality as machinelike with separate parts. Our seminary education is largely divided into parts: systematic theology, church history, biblical studies, and practical disciplines of pastoral care, preaching, and leadership. The individual student, the focus of theological education, is left to integrate the learning from these separate disciplines. Largely absent is a more quantum, systemic, organic worldview that proposes that nothing or no one can be seen as separate and self-contained. Reality is relational. We are always a self *in relationship*. This model, AnamCara, reflects this reality.

[8] I was Director of the Department of Pastoral Care, North Carolina Baptist Hospital, Winston-Salem, NC, 1976–1883.

[9] The root meaning of "Rule" in Latin and Greek is "trellis." Trellis is a framework on which plant life can find its own path within structure. The space in which it moves is open, though not without boundaries. Offering ministry in a culture suspicious of structure and boundaries, "trellis" is an apt metaphor for AnamCara communities. Henry Patrick, editor, *Benedict's Dharma* (The Perkley Publishing Group, 2001), p. 1.

[10] Parker Palmer addresses this need for vocational community. "The growth of any craft depends on shared practice and honest dialogue among the people who do it . . . when any function is privatized, the most likely outcome is that people will perform conservatively refusing to stray far from the silent consensus on what works—even when it clearly does not" *The Courage to Teach* (San Francisco, CA: Jossey-Bass, 1998), p.144.

[11] AnamCara comes from *anam*, the Gaelic word for soul, and *cara*, the word for friend. John O'Donohue, *AnamCara* (New York: HarperCollins Publishers, 1997), p. xviii.

[12] I recommend five to eight participants, large enough for different perspectives and personalities, and small enough for personal attention.

[13] I find it noteworthy that these are the same three essentials of living religion named by lay theologian Friedrich von Hügel (1852–1925) — the institutional (leadership), the intellectual (theological reflection), and mysticism (love of God). Quoted in Dorothee Soelle, *The Silent Cry* (Minneapolis, MN: Fortress Press, 2001), p. 1.

[14] O'Donohue, *op.cit.*, p. 13.

[15] Parker Palmer writes, "We know how to create spaces that invite the *intellect* to show up . . . spaces that invite the *emotions* into play . . . spaces that invite the *will* to emerge . . . spaces that invite the *ego* to put in an appearance . . . But we know very little about creating spaces that invite the *soul* to make itself known and do its work in our midst." *Hidden Wholeness: The Journey toward an Undivided Life* (Jossey-Bass, 2004), p. 56

[16] Pastor, priest, and prophet are not separate identities for me. I understand priest and prophet as expressions of the single identity pastor. The pastor as priest tilts toward the congregation, positioning the pathos of being human within the steadfast love of God. The pastor as prophet tilts toward the world, declaring the pathos of God toward any abuses of living beings, whether human or non-human. Furthermore, prophetic witness is always grounded in community. Such public prophets as Martin Luther King, Jr. can appear as lone heroes when viewed through individualistic lens. In reality, their witness arose from a community of mostly unnamed and unknown colleagues. "Lone prophet" is an oxymoron.

[17] This metaphor of a jam mirrors one from Jack H. Bloom. Bloom wants rabbis (and pastors) to have a place like a backstage in a theater. It is a place where you can let your hair down, share coffee and banter, discuss the play, and say things you would rather not be heard out on the stage. Jack H. Bloom, *The Rabbi as Symbolic Exemplar* (New York: The Haworth Press, 2002), p. 146.

[18] Anthropologist Victor Turner names the transforming power in rituals as "liminality." "Liminal" comes from the Latin word, "limen," meaning threshold. See Tom F. Driver, *The Magic of Ritual* (New York: HarperSanFrancisco, 1991), pp. 157–65.

[19] Robert Bellah and associates write that the individualism in America, so preoccupied with asserting our rights, "leaves the individual suspended in glorious but terrifying isolation." Quoted in Margaret Wheatley, *Leadership and the New Sciences* (San Francisco, CA: Berritt-Koehler Publishers, 1992), p. 6

[20] I am indebted to Jack H. Bloom for so accurately naming this tension. Bloom, *op.cit.*, pp. 135–138.

[21] "A rabbi's private and public life is expected to be a seamless whole marked by the warp of integrity and the woof of caring love." *Ibid.*, p. 154.

[22] David Odum speaks to the difficulty of pastors forming authentic personal relationships with congregants. "Though pastors think of [relationships with members] in a very warm way, it's not a two-way relationship like what you'd have between two close friends . . . You're very close with people, but there's a part of you that you can't share with them." Quoted in an interview by John Hall and Hannah Elliott, Associated Baptist Press, October 4, 2006.

[23] Building community may be more difficult in our day. Gilbert Rendle notes the cultural shift from group identity to individual identity. Drawing from historians William Strauss and Neil Howe, Rendle charts the movement in the last decades

from serving institutions to institutions serving individuals. The values—autonomy, self-expression, and self-self-fulfillment—are primary. The pastor calling for commitment to community is swimming against the cultural stream. Gilbert R. Rendle, *Behavioral Covenants in Congregations* (An Alban Institute Publication, 1999), p. 11.

[24] John Cobb writes, "The renewal of the vocation of theology in the churches will not and cannot come from the professional theologians whose work centers in academia. It can only come from the churches themselves . . . It does require that church people recognize that unless we reflect seriously, as Christians, about who we are and what we are called to be we continue to drift into decadence." John Cobb, *Reclaiming the Church* (Louisville, KY: Westminster John Knox Press, 1997), p. 31.

[25] Canadian theologian Douglas John Hall challenges pastors to be thinkers. "Theology, which throughout most of its history has been regarded as the rarified occupation of a small minority of scholars, is now the responsibility of the whole church . . . Our churches do not need managers, they need thinkers! They need people whose knowledge of the Scriptures, traditions, and contemporary Christian (religious) scholarship is more deeply developed than has been required of clergy in the past. They need teachers, resident theologians, teaching elders, rabbis; learned persons who can prevent the faith from being reduced to platitudes and ethical truisms . . . Ours is a time for prophetic ministry, not for 'pastoral directors." Douglas John Hall, *Confessing the Faith* (Minneapolis, MN: Fortress Press, 1998), p. 195.

[26] A few examples of statements from seers:

"[We are at] a critical moment in Earth's history, a time when humanity must choose its future . . . one human family and one Earth community with a common destiny." The Earth Charter (2000), quoted in David Korten, *The Great Turning* (San Francisco, CA: Kumarian Press, 2006), p. 3.

"I think there are good reasons for suggesting that the modern age has ended. Today, many things indicate that we are going through a transitional period when it seems that something is on the way out and something else is painfully being born." Vaclav Havel, former president of the Czech Republic on the occasion of the Library Medal Ceremony, Philadelphia, July 4, 1994.

"Christianity has arrived at the end of its sojourn as the official, or established, religion of the Western world . . . The end of Christendom could be the beginning of something more nearly like the church—the disciple community described by the Scriptures and treasured throughout the ages by prophetic minorities." Hall, *The End of Christendom and the Future of Christianity* (Harrisburg, PA: Trinity Press International, 1995), p. 51.

"[The church is] in the awkwardly intermediate stage of having once been culturally established but . . . not yet clearly disestablished." George Lindbeck, *The Nature of Doctrine*, p. 134, quoted in Hall, *ibid.*, p. 53.

[27] Gil Rendle, "Leadership Under Constraints," a paper prepared for the leadership of The United Methodist Church, 2006, pp. 3–5.

[28] Another compelling image of transition comes from columnist Thomas Friedman. "We are all pilgrims again, sailing on the Mayflower anew. We have not

been to this shore before. If we fail to recognize that, we will, indeed become just one more endangered species. But if we arise to the challenge and truly become the Re-generation—re-defining green and discovering, reviving, and regenerating America—we, and the world, will not only survive but thrive in an age that is hot, flat and crowded." Thomas L. Friedman, *Hot, Flat, and Crowded* (New York: Farrar, Straus and Giroux, 2008), p. 412.

[29] Edwin H. Friedman, *A Failure of Nerve: Leadership in the Age of the Quick-fix* (New York: Seabury Books, 2007), pp. 51–94.

[30] Roy Oswald, a consultant for The Alban Institute, with long consulting experience "advised that the category of 'spiritual leadership,' including the defining and sharing of vision, should take 40% of the time spent by an effective leader." Quoted in Wesley Granberg-Michaelson, *Leadership From the Inside Out* (New York: Crossroad Publishing Company, 2004), p.108.

[31] This metaphor of leadership of getting off the dance floor and going to the balcony is from Ronald A. Heifetz and Marty Linsky, *Leadership on the Line* (Boston, MA: Harvard Business School Press, 2002), p. 51.

[32] This work of self-understanding as leader includes exposure to various theories of leadership. Leadership from a family systems perspective as defined by Edwin Friedman has been the theory active in my AnamCara work. A narrative approach to pastoral leadership is powerfully articulated by Richard L. Hester and Kelli Walker-Jones in their book, *Know Your Story And Lead With It* published by The Alban Institute, available in fall, 2009. Facilitators, along with their AnamCara group, will decide what theoretical lens to use. The goal is to help each pastor, by drawing on both theory and practice with peers, to clarify how they define themselves as leaders.

[33] Barbara Brown Taylor speaks to this experience in her life. "My role and my soul were eating each other alive. I wanted out of the belief business and back into the beholding business . . . Because I did not know to give my soul what it wanted, I continued to play my role, becoming more brittle with every passing day." Barbara Brown Taylor, *Leaving Church* (San Francisco, CA: HarperSanFrancisco, 2006), p. 111.

[34] Luke 10: 27; I John 4: 19

[35] Henri Nouwen describes his loss of soul. "Everyone was saying I was doing really well, but something inside was telling me that my success was putting my own soul in danger . . . I woke up one day with the realization that I was living in a very dark place and that the term 'burnout' was a convenient, psychological translation for a spiritual death." Henri Nouwen, *In the Name of Jesus* (New York: Crossroad Publishing Company, 1989), pp. 10, 11.

[36] My idealism focused me outward in activity, away from the nurture of inner resources. Walter Wink, in his trilogy on Powers, positions faithfulness as up against suprahuman forces that diminish our humanity and reduces us to prayer. "Unprotected by prayer, our social activism [and pastoral ministry] run[s] the danger of becoming self-justifying good works, as our inner resources atrophy [and] the wells of love run dry. Walter Wink, *Engaging the Powers* (Minneapolis, MN: Fortress Press, 1992), p. 298.

[37] Galatians 2: 19–20

[38] Some of us take advantage of resources that enhance self-awareness, such as psychotherapy, pastoral counseling, body work, the Myers-Briggs Indicator, the family geneogram, and the Enneagram to name a few.

[39] Cynthia Bourgeault makes a distinction between psychotherapy as a way of healing the ego and spiritual inner work as a way of transcending self. "Classic psychotherapy takes place with the domain of egoic functioning; its goal is to improve it. Through therapy, wounded and dysfunctional people get the help they need to live better-adjusted and more successful lives . . . Classic spiritual work, no matter what the religious tradition, is about transcending ego . . . This does not necessarily mean eliminating the ego, but rather displacing it as the seat of one's personal identity. The process is rather like discovering that the earth revolves around the sun rather than vice versa." Cynthia Bourgeault, *Centering Prayer and Inner Awakening* (Cambridge, MA: Cowley Publications, 2004), p. 102.

[40] Bourgeault adds these comments to the question of identity. "Jesus taught from the conviction that we human beings are victims of a tragic case of mistaken identity. The person I normally take myself to be—that busy anxious little 'I' so preoccupied with its goals, fears, desires, and issues—is never even remotely the whole of who I am, and to seek the fulfillment of my life at this level means to miss out on the bigger life . . . Beneath the surface there is a deeper and vastly more authentic Self, but its presence is usually veiled by the clamor of the smaller 'I' with its insatiable needs and demands." *Ibid.*, p. 10.

[41] "We are what we repeatedly do. Excellence, therefore, is not an act, but a habit." Aristotle

[42] "Every dynamic new force for change is undergirded by rigorous disciplines. The slack decadence of culture-Christianity cannot produce athletes of the spirit. Those who are bearers of tomorrow undergo what others might call disciplines, but not to punish themselves or to ingratiate themselves to God. They simply do what is necessary to stay spiritually alive, just as they eat food and drink water." Wink, *op.cit.*, p. 261.

[43] Of these three, accountability is the least understood and most neglected. In comparison with most professionals, we are loosely accountable to others, including our congregation. We are largely left to ourselves with minimal accountability.

Accountability raises the question of community: How are we doing with the promises we have made, both to ourselves and to each other? These circles of trust grant the safety to confess broken promises, explore resistances to promise-keeping, and celebrate and build upon promises kept. Accountability favors curious questions not answers, honest feedback not critical analysis, challenge nor hard judgment. Without effective accountability, the group, as with any community, will plateau, then falter.

[44] I am told that the infamous Ted Williams counseled, "If you are in a slump, don't try to swing harder. Change your stance!"

[45] John Scherer, "The Role of Chaos in the Creation of Change," *Creative Change* vol. 12, no. 2 (Spring, 1991), pp. 19–29.

Appendix I

Responses to Questions

I have tried clergy groups. They didn't last. How will this be different?

I appreciate the realism in the question. Creating and sustaining a trustworthy community can look deceptively simple. From other attempts with small groups, we know the complexity involved. Some just don't work, likely due to a combination of factors—lack of clear covenants, inadequate structure and leadership, competition, control struggles, unwillingness to risk vulnerability and accountability or just plain absence of "chemistry." The challenges of intimacy, experienced by us in other relationships, will, of course, be present in vocational friendships. We fall back to a familiar truth: community is always a mystery, more gift than achievement.

But having acknowledged the mystery, I want to affirm the benefits of the four extended AnamCara groups I co-led, plus the two on-going groups in the Washington D.C. area that I observe from a distance. I suspect the "difference" in value from many clergy groups stems from these factors: its organic nature from integrating four practices fundamental to pastoral ministry; the attention to clear covenants at the beginning; skilled facilitators committed to the model; facilitators who have experience as pastors; common worship; flexible structure, balance between silence and word; and the movement from collegiality to friendships. CareNet has plans to conduct professional research of AnamCara groups during this initial phase from which we hope to learn more about the "difference."

What do you mean by "on-going" community?

Most programs for continuing education that include peer groups are short term, two or three years at the longest, with participants returning to a solo model of ministry. I envision a continuing community with annual opportunities for participants to withdraw and include new members. A period of a year grants the time to live into this different way of doing ministry and evaluate its worth.

I recognize that the mobility of clergy is a challenge to continuity. Perhaps, if AnamCara is life-giving, those moving to other places could be instrumental in forming new clergy communities. This has already happened.

This all sounds interesting, but here's my major question: how much time are we talking about?

Time is our principal currency in ministry, and for good reason we protect and spend it carefully. Giving time means giving presence and investing energy. A "yes" to these relationships carries a "no" to other options. I would expect the commitment of time to be a critical consideration.

During the ten years of developing this vision, I have experimented with the time required to move from an individualized ministry to a ministry nurtured within a small circle of collegial friends. I have asked: How much time together is necessary to foster the trust and commitment required in an on-going community?

This is the amount of time I recommend. The commitment involves two stages.

> **Stage I:** Along with the other five to eight pastors, you would commit to an initial **two-day retreat** for the purpose of forming a covenant (see Appendix III). The retreat would be designed to include experiences with each of the four practices: becoming community; theological reflection and discernment; case presentation on leadership; and silence, prayer, worship. Practical matters, such as how monthly gatherings would be facilitated, where the group would meet, schedule for meetings, rules (like confidentiality) would be decided during this retreat.
>
> Someone experienced in this model would facilitate this retreat. Following this retreat, with covenant agreements clearer,

AnamCara — Collegial Clergy Communities

each person will make a final decision to commit or not to commit.

Stage II: Assuming the covenanting was formed in the initial retreat, the minimal commitment of time for gathering together includes:

1) One **full day a month** (8:30–4:00) designed to address the four areas of practicing: becoming community; theological reflection/discernment; consultation around leadership; and prayer and worship. The day will also include ample unstructured time, for after all, this is a gathering of friends (see Appendix III for sample).

2) In addition, during the weeks when the community is not meeting for the full day, each AnamCara will determine a way to be together, perhaps around a meal, coffee, e-mails, blogs, or conference calls. I am aware of one clergy group of friends who e-mail one another every Monday morning reflecting about the previous day of worship or previous week. This informal, unstructured time allows for checking-in with each other and provides the occasion for specific support or collaboration if needed. Mostly it is time apart to enjoy one another and deepen friendships. This means that the community would make contact each week of the month. This Stage II commitment will be for a year. At the annual mark, perhaps during a retreat, there is time for evaluation including the opportunity for clergy to leave the community and for new clergy to join.

What about the impact on my family?

With such an intentional investment in a few relationships, other primary relationships will be affected. Positively, having a place for personal renewal and professional support and consultation might enable a higher level of presence with spouses and children. Negatively, these collegial relationships might be experienced as competitors for intimacy.

Previously a few of the collegial groups worked at ways to include spouses. One group included a marriage enrichment event. Others met for occasional social gatherings in each other's home. Of course, each circle will address this concern in its own way.

Should the congregation be involved?

There are good reasons for at least the leaders of the congregation to be involved. Certainly they need to support your commitment of time. More so, I hope they would see this as a gift, not just to your self-care, but a gift to your leadership of the congregation. I find that most lay leaders observe the stresses in pastoral ministry and welcome ways for their pastors to strengthen themselves both personally and professionally.

Appendix II

The Covenant of AnamCara: Collegial Clergy Communities

Within a community of 5–8 pastors, plus facilitator(s), clergy colleagues commit to offer support, collaboration, and accountability to these practices:

- The practice of forming and sustaining a community of trust
- The practice of theological reflection and discernment
- The practice of reviewing one's leadership in consultation with peers
- Practices of prayer and worship
- The practice of presence at the gatherings of the AnamCara community:

Beginning with a **Two-day Covenanting Retreat**

Monthly meeting — a full day scheduled by each community

Weekly meetings — during the weeks when the community does meet for the full day, the circle connects in ways of their own choosing (breakfast, lunch, coffee or through the internet)

Annual retreat — for evaluation, celebration, and either renewal or termination of the community.

Appendix III

Designing Time

How we use our time is another way to introduce the AnamCara vision.

AnamCara is a process of practicing within a community of peers. Though each community of five to eight clergy will give shape to its own life together, the consistent focus of all the communities are the four practices: building and sustaining community; theological reflecting and discerning; attending to the leadership of a congregation; and through prayer and worship re-centering our lives and ministry in God's grace and power.

How might these gatherings be designed?

I. The Covenanting Retreat

AnamCara begins with a two-day retreat. Participants will clarify how they want to be together in community. The facilitator, trained in the model of AnamCara, will lead the retreat. The retreat is designed to allow participants to *experience* the core practices of AnamCara.

In different ways, the retreat addresses these questions:

- How will we build and sustain our community?
- How will we engage in theological reflection and discernment?
- How will we review our leadership of our congregations?
- How will we engage collectively in spiritual practices and also support the spiritual practices of each person?
- When and where will we meet?

II. **The Monthly Day**

The full day each month is designed to include all four practices: forming and sustaining a community of trust; theological reflection and discernment; reviewing one's leadership; and contemplative prayer and worship. Such a day might look like this:

8:15 – 9:00   **brief check-in**

9:00 – 10:15   **lectio divina** (fifteen minutes reading a scripture passage three times with pauses in between; thirty minutes of silence with participants free to be by themselves; and thirty minutes of sharing from the experience.)

10:15 – 10:30   **break**

10:30 – 11:30   **case presentation**

11:30 – 1:00   **lunch/rest/walk**

1:00 – 2:15   **reflecting theologically on the mission/vocation of the church** (book or article discussion, film, etc.)

2:15 – 3:30   **open time** (depending on the needs/desires of group, this is time for further sharing of personal/work concerns or walking/resting or alone time for personal reflecting or playing together, etc.)

3:30 – 3:45   **accessing the day,** including review of promises made around personal disciplines for which the group offers support and accountability.

3:45 – 4:30   **closing worship** (e.g. Communion)

III. **The Weekly Meeting** (during the weeks when the circle does not meet for the full day.)

The purpose of this time is two-fold: checking in with each other and enjoying the friendships. The gathering might be around coffee/tea, breakfast, lunch, or some other way of being in touch.

Appendix IV

A Model of Case Presentation

This form of case presentation involves a presenter, a partner and a reflecting team of five or six. It invites deep listening and curious questions so that the presenter can reflect on internal clarities and options, and not be caught up in reacting to others' comments or advice. This model I learned from Richard L. Hester and Kelli Walker-Jones. A fuller description can be found in their book, *Know Your Story,* published by Alban Institute, Fall, 2009.

> **20 minutes**—the presenter shares a leadership incident (guidelines will be provided) with the listening partner. The partner's responsibilities are (1) to listen with curiosity; (2) to ask curious questions that focus on the inner world and responses of the presenter, not so much on the other persons in the situation presented.
>
> **15 minutes**—the reflecting team talks among themselves about what they have overheard, keeping the focus of their conversation on the presenter, not the details of the leadership incident. The presenter and partner step back and overhear their conversation.
>
> **10 minutes**—The presenter responds in conversation with the listening partner about what has been overheard from the reflecting team that seems pertinent to her or his learning.
>
> **15 minutes**—The boundaries are removed so all join in the conversation which includes theological reflection. Personal insights regarding leadership are noted.